The Life of Jesus

Adapted from the Gospels
According to Matthew and John

By Pamela Broughton
Illustrated by Joy Friedman

A GOLDEN BOOK® • NEW YORK

A long time ago, a man named John heard good
news from God. God's Son was coming to live on earth.

John went through the country, telling people the
news. The people believed the news. They followed John
to the River Jordan. There John baptized them in the
water.

One day Jesus came to be baptized. Jesus was John's cousin.

When John saw Jesus, he said, "This is the Son of God."

After He was baptized, Jesus went into the desert to pray. There He met the devil.

Jesus had no food in the desert. He went forty days without eating. The devil tempted Him, saying, "If You are the Son of God, change these stones to bread."

But Jesus said, "Man does not live by bread alone."

The devil showed Jesus all the kingdoms of the world. He said, "Serve me, and You will rule the world."

But Jesus said, "You shall worship the Lord your God and serve Him only."

The devil took Jesus to the top of the Temple at Jerusalem. "Jump off," he said. "God will not allow His Son to be hurt." But Jesus would not.

He told the devil, "God says, 'Do not test Me.'"

The devil saw that he could not make Jesus serve him. So the devil sneaked away until a better time. And angels came and helped Jesus.

Then Jesus returned home and began to teach the Word of God. News about Him spread through the country.

Some men who heard the news decided to follow Jesus. They were called disciples. Their names were John, James, Andrew, Peter, Philip, Nathanael, Thomas, Matthew, Simon, Thaddeus, and James, the son of Alphaeus.

Another man decided to follow Jesus, too. His name was Judas.

The disciples learned about God from Jesus, and they helped Jesus teach others.

Now there were people called Pharisees who did
not like the things Jesus said. They wanted to stop Him
from teaching. But they could not stop His followers
from spreading news of the wonderful things Jesus did.

One day, Jesus went to a wedding in a small town called Cana. During the celebration, the wine ran out.

Jesus told the servants to fill six stone jars with water. Then He told them to pour some out. The water had turned to wine, and there was enough for all the guests.

After this, Jesus and His disciples were at the pool of Siloam. There lived a man who had been born blind.

Jesus spat on the ground to make clay. He put the clay on the man's eyes and told him to wash in the pool. The man did what Jesus said. When he came back, he could see.

The man was brought before the Pharisees. They said to him, "This Jesus only pretends to be from God. He is nothing more than a magician who does wicked tricks."

But the man said, "I only know that I was blind, and now I see. If Jesus were not from God, He could not make me see."

But the Pharisees wanted to punish Jesus.

Jesus heard that His friend Lazarus was very sick. After two days, Jesus said, "Lazarus is dead now. But I will wake him."

The disciples were afraid. They knew the Pharisees would punish them if they heard any more about Jesus' "tricks."

But Jesus was not afraid. When He reached His friend's house, Lazarus's sister ran out to meet Him.

"Lord," she said, "if You had been here, my brother would not have died. Even now, I know that God will grant whatever You ask."

Jesus said, "Your brother shall rise again."

They went to Lazarus's grave. They removed the stone
that covered the grave, and Jesus prayed to God. Then
Jesus said, "Lazarus, come forth!"
Lazarus came out of the grave. He was alive!

Then many people believed that Jesus was from God. But the devil saw that a better time had come and that his evil could succeed. He told Judas to go to the Pharisees. Now Judas was not a good man, as the other disciples were. So he listened to the devil. He told the Pharisees that he would help them arrest Jesus.

Jesus and His disciples were in the garden of Gethsemane. The Pharisees sent Judas there with soldiers to take Jesus away.

Jesus was beaten, and a crown of thorns was placed on His head. Then He was nailed to a cross.

After Jesus had hung on the cross for nine hours, the sky grew dark. Jesus said, "It is finished," and He died.

His followers took His body away for burial.

Two days later, some of Jesus' friends went to pray by Jesus' tomb. They were surprised by what they found—the stone that covered the tomb had been removed, and the tomb was empty.

An angel sat before the tomb. He said, "Do not be afraid. I know that you are looking for Jesus, but He is not here. He has risen. You will see Him and speak with Him again."

The disciples were overjoyed when they met Jesus, the risen Lord. Jesus taught the disciples more about God's love.

"Rejoice!" He said. "For I am with you always, even to the end of the world."